THE HISTORY OF
COMMUNICATION

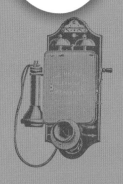

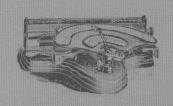

Michael Woods and Mary B. Woods

TFCB TWENTY-FIRST CENTURY BOOKS

Minneapolis

To Alexander Charles Woods who communicated such joy and wonder to us.

Twenty-First Century Books
A division of Lerner Publishing Group
241 First Avenue North
Minneapolis, MN 55401 U.S.A.

Website address: www.lernerbooks.com

Library of Congress Cataloging-in-Publication Data

Woods, Michael, 1946–
    The history of communication / by Michael and Mary B. Woods.
        p.   cm. — (Major inventions through history)
    Includes bibliographical references and index.
    ISBN-13: 978–0–8225–3807–3 (lib. bdg. : alk. paper)
    ISBN-10: 0–8225–3807–5 (lib. bdg. : alk. paper)
      1. Communication—History—Juvenile literature. I. Woods, Mary B. (Mary
Boyle), 1946– II. Title. III. Series.
    P91.2.W593 2006
    302.2'09-dc22   2005013993

Manufactured in the United States of America
1 2 3 4 5 6 – DP – 11 10 09 08 07 06

CONTENTS

Introduction

One thousand years ago, sharing information was very difficult. Books cost a lot of money because there was no quick or easy way to print them. Few people ever saw a book. As a result, most people never learned to read. Sharing information fast with people who lived far away was just a dream.

Inventions, created and improved over centuries, changed that situation. Inventions made it easier for people to communicate, or share information. People used new inventions such as telephones and radio to communicate with each other. The inventions became so important that life without them is hard to imagine. Just try to imagine life without telephones, TV, or the Internet!

In this book, you will discover amazing methods of communication. They allowed people to get more information easier and faster. They put information from all over the world right at our fingertips.

CHAPTER 1

The Printing Press

Up until the 1400s, there was only one way to make books. Workers called scribes created books by hand. They wrote down words onto blank sheets of parchment, a paperlike material made from the skin of sheep, goats, or calves. When they were done writing, the scribes gathered the sheets together into books. These books were called manuscripts, which means "written by hand."

Scribes wrote each letter with a quill, the sharpened tip of a feather. They dipped the tip into a pot of ink. Dip. Write one letter. Dip again. Write another. They left space for pictures. An artist drew the pictures by hand with colored ink.

Scribes often copied books from ancient Greece or Rome, or religious books such as the Bible. Looking at the old book, a scribe wrote the words one at a time on a fresh sheet of parchment. Because each page was large and packed with many words, it took a scribe about one day to write one page. Sometimes it took years to finish just one book. A scribe might produce only a few books in an entire lifetime.

Books were expensive to make and precious to own. Only the richest people could afford to own even one. In the 800s, Europe's biggest library was in Saint Gall, Switzerland. It had an amazing thirty-six books!

THE TYPEWRITER

Handwriting can be sloppy and sometimes hard to read. Writing by hand is also slow. In the 1870s, the invention of the typewriter allowed people to print out letters, stories, and other written works without writing by hand. Instead of writing, people pressed keys on a type-writer, which printed letters and numbers on a sheet of paper. For more than one hundred years, people used typewriters in homes, schools, and businesses. In the twenty-first century, however, type-writers are rare, because people use computer keyboards and print-ers instead.

Movable Type

In the mid-1400s, German inventor Johannes Gutenberg began building a printing press, a machine to print books fast. Gutenberg's printing press included small metal blocks called type. Each piece of type had a raised letter, number, or other character on the upper end. Inside a wooden frame, Gutenberg lined up the blocks to form words, sort of like tiles in the board game Scrabble. The words were arranged into sentences.

When Gutenberg had set up enough type for a page, he rolled ink over the type. He placed a sheet of paper on top of the inked type, then turned a screw to press a block of wood against the paper onto the type. Ink from the type stuck to the paper and printed out the words. By repeating the process over and over, Gutenberg's press could

PRINTING WITH WOOD AND CLAY

Johannes Gutenberg did not invent printing. People in China and Japan used carved wooden blocks to print pictures and letters hundreds of years before Gutenberg. They applied ink to the blocks and then pressed them onto paper, creating printed images.

Around A.D. 1045, Chinese printer Bi Sheng invented an early form of movable type. He carved each character, which stood for a word or part of a word, into a block of clay. But the Chinese language has thousands of different characters. So it was nearly impossible for Bi Sheng to make all the blocks he needed. His blocks also broke easily and could be reused only a few times.

A Chinese printer creates the first movable type.

A.D. 1045

Johannes Gutenberg builds a printing press that uses movable type.

1440s

This engraving depicts Johannes Gutenberg *(far right)* inspecting the first page proof off his printing press. To imprint type onto a page, a printer turned a large screw that flattened the inked type against the paper.

make hundreds of copies of each page. Instead of the scribe making only one page a day, Gutenberg could print one page every three minutes.

After printing many copies of a page, Gutenberg could take the lines of type apart (which is why we call it movable type). Then he rearranged the type to spell out words for the next page.

Changing People's Lives

Gutenberg's invention soon changed the way people lived. Because the printing press made it cheaper and easier to make books, the price of books began to drop. Ordinary people could finally afford books. More people learned to read. People used printing presses to make newspapers too.

The printing press made it possible for people to learn about places far away from their hometowns. They could discover how other people lived. Storybooks about fictional events entertained people and let them imagine and dream.

FAST FACT

In 1791 the First Amendment to the U.S. Constitution provided for freedom of the press. Freedom of the press means that people can publish facts, ideas, and opinions in newspapers, books, and electronic media without the government stopping them or telling them what to say.

Speedier Printing

In the mid-1800s, inventors made presses that could print faster. One was the rotary printing press. It was shaped like a cylinder, or drum, with lines of type around the outside. The rotary press printed words on long rolls of paper, turning out thousands of printed sheets per hour. With better presses, books and newspapers could be printed at an even lower cost. More and more people could afford to buy them.

The First Amendment to the U.S. Constitution grants Americans freedom of the press.
1791

E. Remington and Sons produces the first commercial typewriter.
1821

Even with faster presses, type was still set by hand. It was a slow process. It took two printers two or three days to assemble enough type for just a few newspaper pages. German American inventor Ottmar Mergenthaler sped up the process in 1884. He invented the Linotype machine to do the job automatically. The Linotype operator sat at a keyboard and typed in the text to be printed. The machine changed the keystrokes into lines of type. It

This Linotype printer was the first model made by Mergenthaler Linotype Company. It was first used by the *New York Tribune* in 1886.

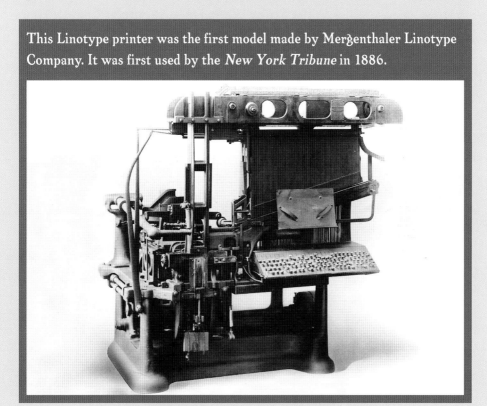

allowed printers to set several pages of newspaper type in a few hours rather than a few days.

Printing the Modern World

Until the early 1900s, most printing was done by Gutenberg's letterpress method, which involved pressing inked type against paper. In 1904 a faster and less expensive kind of printing was invented. It was called offset printing because no direct contact occurred between the inked type and the paper. Instead, the inked image was offset, or transferred, onto a rubber-coated cylinder, then onto paper.

Offset printing was among many inventions that allowed more lifelike pictures and photographs to be printed in newspapers and other publications. New inventions also made it easy to print full-color pictures. Modern printing presses are complex, high-powered machines. They can print almost one hundred thousand copies of a newspaper in one hour.

BOOKS WITHOUT PAPER

E-books, or electronic books, are books you can download from the Internet. Go to www.ebooks.com to find a catalog. With e-books, the whole book is a computer file, just like the files you create for school reports. You can read an e-book right on your computer monitor. Just scroll down from line to line. Or you can print the book on your home computer printer. It costs money to print out e-books. People pay for this online using credit cards.

U.S. printers begin using offset printing.
1904

Your One-Million-Dollar Printing Press

Do you have an ink-jet printer at home? Many families have one. They often cost less than two hundred dollars. Ink-jets are light and small. But ink-jets print beautiful color pictures and sharp, clear words. Until the late 1900s, there was only one way to get such printing. You'd have to buy a one-million-dollar printing press. It was bigger than a truck.

HA HA!

Question: "What's black and white and read all over?"
Answer: "The newspaper!"

New inventions such as ink-jet and laser printers keep the information revolution rolling ahead. Johannes Gutenberg never could have dreamed of them. What do you think printing will be like in the twenty-second century?

CHAPTER 2

The Telephone

A world with no telephones? It's hard to imagine. Have you ever gone for a day without using the phone—perhaps when storms knocked down the telephone wires? You couldn't stay in touch with your friends, make plans, or share ideas and feelings.

That was everyday life up until the late 1800s. Until then, when people wanted to share thoughts with others, they usually sent letters. The postal service was slow. Weeks might pass before a letter

American inventor Samuel F. B. Morse makes the first usable telegraph.

1837

writer received a reply from someone in another city. People could not telephone the police for help in an emergency. They could not save time by shopping or getting information over the phone. Friends who moved to different cities might never hear each other's voices again.

A woman in Chicago, Illinois, who wanted to contact her brother in Boston, Massachusetts—fast—had only one option: sending a telegram. She went to a building called the telegraph office and stood in line. She told an operator what she wanted to say.

A telegraph operator takes down a message.

The United States has more than fifty telegraph companies.

1851

The operator typed out the message in code by tapping on a button. This process turned the message into electrical signals, which traveled, in less than a second, over wires that stretched from Chicago to Boston. In Boston another telegraph operator translated the coded message into words and wrote it down. A messenger then delivered the letter in person. Sending a message this way was expensive.

A Race to the Patent Office

Alexander Graham Bell and U.S. inventor Elisha Gray both applied for patents on their telephones on February 14, 1876. A patent is a certificate issued by the U.S. government that says which person has the right to make and sell a new invention.

Bell got the patent, because he applied for it two hours before Gray did. That's one reason Bell usually gets credit for inventing the telephone. Bell's telephone also worked better than Gray's, and Bell kept improving his telephone. His telephone system soon came to lead the telephone industry in the United States.

Phone Home

British scientist Michael Faraday had a big role in inventing the telephone. In 1831 he had discovered that sounds made a thin piece of metal vibrate, or flutter. He figured out how the vibrations could be changed into electrical signals. In Boston Alexander Graham Bell used Faraday's discovery to invent the telephone in 1876.

The word *telephone* means "talking from a distance." A telephone changes the human voice

Alexander Graham Bell
invents the telephone.
1876

into electric signals. The signals travel over a wire or cable (or through the air in the case of modern cell phones) to another telephone. The second phone changes the electric signals into sounds that are just like the originals.

The First Telephones

Early telephones were not like modern phones. They were big and heavy. The phone was connected to the wall by a short wire, so users could not walk around while talking on the phone. The first phones had no dial or keypad. The caller picked up the receiver and gave a phone number to an operator working in an office. The operator then dialed the number and connected the call through a switchboard.

With early telephones, voices could be fuzzy, low, and hard to hear. Sometimes phone lines got "crossed," and callers could hear other people's phone conversations in the background. Connections got cut off in the middle of calls too. Sometimes several houses in the same area shared a phone line, called a party line. Neighbors could pick up the phone and listen to someone

THE FIRST PHONE CALL

A famous story says that the first real telephone call took place on March 10, 1876. Alexander Graham Bell was working alone in a room. He yelled to his assistant, Thomas Watson, in another room, "Mr. Watson—come here—I want to see you." Watson heard the request through a telephone connected to equipment in Bell's room. At that moment, history was made.

U.S. president Rutherford B. Hayes calls Alexander Graham Bell from a telephone in the White House.

1878

SORE FINGERS!

Early telephone numbers were short. You could call a friend by dialing just four numbers, such as 3760. Numbers began to run out as more Americans got telephones. So telephone companies assigned people longer numbers, so there would be more combinations of numbers to go around. By the 1960s, phone numbers had seven digits. You'd have to dial 555-3760 to reach that friend. If the friend lived in another city, you'd have to dial a three-digit area code first. That meant ten numbers, such as 555-555-3760, to talk with that friend. In modern times, we often have to dial ten numbers even to reach friends who live nearby. If you want to call a friend in another country, you might have to dial fifteen numbers!

else's call. Making a long-distance call was very expensive.

Eventually, inventors made telephones easier to use. They invented phones with dials and keypads that allowed users to place calls without the help of an operator.

Phones Get Better

The United States started with just one phone system. It was called the Bell Telephone Company, after Alexander Graham Bell. The system included wires and special switches to carry electronic signals. At first, telephone wires were made of copper. Each pair of copper wires could carry only one phone conversation at a time. It took thousands of wires to connect all the phones in a town.

In 1937 inventors figured out how to send hundreds of conversations over just one pair of wires. This invention made phone

The Bell Telephone System shuts down for one minute after the death of Alexander Graham Bell.

1922

Telephone companies create area codes for placing long-distance calls.

1951

systems more efficient. In the 1970s, inventors created optical fibers, hair-thin threads of glass (later plastic) that could carry information on beams of light. In modern phone systems, two strands of fiber, barely big enough to see, can carry twenty-four thousand telephone calls at one time.

Telephones kept improving. Inventors developed call waiting, caller ID, and call forwarding. They created conference calling, which allows more than two callers to talk together as a group. In the

A single 4.5-pound (2-kilogram) roll of optical fiber can carry as many phone calls as a roll of copper wire weighing 1,600 pounds (726 kg)!

Inventors develop
touch-tone phones.
1963

FUN FACTS ABOUT PHONES

- In 1878 Rutherford B. Hayes became the first U.S. president to use a telephone in the White House. Who got his first call? Alexander Graham Bell.

- After Alexander Graham Bell died on August 2, 1922, all phones in the Bell Telephone System also died—but for just one minute. The system was shut down for a moment of silence in Bell's honor.

- All telephones had a rotary dial until 1963. The dial was a little wheel with numbered holes. You put a finger in a hole and spun the wheel to dial each digit of the phone number. Touch-tone phones, invented in 1963, were faster and saved wear and tear on the fingers.

- In the early twenty-first century, people in the United States were using more than 170 million cell phones.

late 1900s, inventors discovered more ways to use telephone lines. Fax machines, for instance, can send pictures over telephone lines. People also connect to the Internet over telephone lines.

Cell phones are the latest advancement in telephones. Cell phones allow people to communicate using radio signals instead of telephone lines. Some cell phones can send e-mail messages and connect to the Internet.

Changing People's Lives

Telephones have changed everyday life in countless ways. Telephones save time and allow us to work faster. We can call and order a pizza, for instance, rather than driving to the pizza parlor. In an emergency, we can get help fast by dialing 911. Modern telephones allow you to

U.S. phone users can order caller ID service.

1995

You might think that cell phones *(right)* are brand-new inventions, but police officers actually began using cell phones in patrol cars in the 1920s. These phones were called radio telephones because they used radio signals instead of telephone wires.

call people anywhere, even on the other side of the earth. You can make calls from almost anyplace, even from an airplane.

CHAPTER 3

Radio

Have you ever heard people say "One good thing leads to another"? This saying is especially true for inventions. Most inventions build on existing ideas and improve them. Modern radio, which sends the human voice, music, and other familiar sounds whizzing directly through the air, was based on the earlier inventions of the telegraph and the telephone.

Who Invented Radio?

The Italian inventor Guglielmo Marconi (1874–1937) played a big role in inventing radio. But he based his work on ideas and inventions

of many others, whose names are not well known. In the 1860s, for instance, James Clerk Maxwell, a Scottish scientist, predicted the existence of invisible, naturally occurring radio waves. In 1886

German scientist Heinrich Hertz showed that electric current could be sent through the air in the form of radio waves.

One of the most important inventors in the history of radio was Serbian American Nikola Tesla. Tesla invented a special spool, or coil, of wire. It changed electricity into waves that could travel long distances through the air. In 1895 the Tesla coil transmitted radio waves for 50 miles (80 kilometers). Marconi later used a similar coil in his own long-distance radio transmissions.

Nikola Tesla

Making Waves

The world really began paying attention to radio in 1901, when Marconi transmitted a radio signal across the Atlantic Ocean, from Cornwall, England, to Saint John's, Canada.

Nikola Tesla invents the Tesla coil.
1895

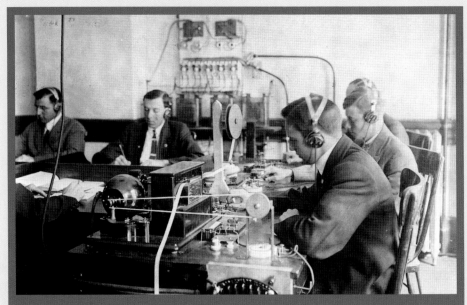

Students learn how to use radio equipment at the Marconi Wireless School in New York City in 1912.

This first transatlantic radio transmission was not the sound of a voice. It consisted of three beeps that stood for the letter *s* in Morse code, the code used to send telegraph messages.

The transmission was a sensation, and it made Marconi very famous. It also made businesspeople realize that radio had a big future. People began investing money in Marconi's radio company. The money allowed Marconi and his staff to do more research and to invent better radio devices.

Guglielmo Marconi sends
the first transatlantic radio
message.
1901

Tuning in to Radio

Sailors were among the first people to use radios. Radios enabled them to communicate with people on distant ships and onshore. In 1912 *Titanic*, a famous passenger ship, hit an iceberg in the Atlantic Ocean and began to sink. *Titanic* had a radio, which sailors used to send out a coded message for help. Another ship, *Carpathia*, also had a radio. Its sailors heard the beep, beep, beeps

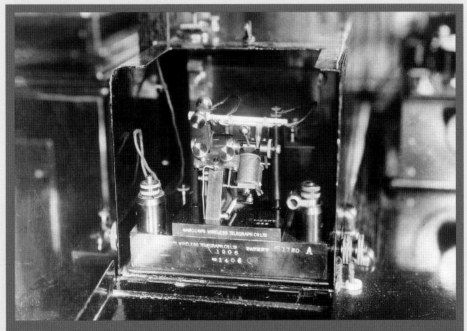

The Marconi wireless radio on which the *Carpathia* received *Titanic's* distress call

Titanic uses its radio to alert nearby ships that it needs help.

1912

sent by *Titanic* and steamed toward the sinking ship. *Carpathia* was able to rescue about seven hundred passengers from *Titanic*. However, about fifteen hundred other passengers died.

Your Grandparents' Television

Radio caused a big change in everyday life in 1920. That's when station KDKA in Pittsburgh, Pennsylvania, began the first regular public radio broadcasts. By 1923 almost six hundred other stations were broadcasting news, music, sports, and other programs.

A woman listens to a Radiola Super VIII radio in 1925. Radio transmitters once weighed more than 100 pounds (45 kg). In modern times, a transmitter can fit on a chip the size of a postage stamp!

Station KDKA in Pittsburgh, Pennsylvania, makes the first commercial radio broadcast.

1920

Soon almost every house in the United States had a radio. Entire families would gather around the radio at night to listen to programs. Nobody wanted to miss a favorite show, especially the serials such as *Tarzan* and *Buck Rogers in the 25th Century*. These ongoing programs often ended on a cliffhanger, with the hero in trouble. Listeners had to tune in to the next show to find out what would happen. Radios also broadcast information about wars, accidents, politics, and other current events.

Making Modern Radio

The first radios were big and heavy, almost the size of a kitchen stove. They also were very expensive. The sound was crackly, with a lot of hisses and static.

But inventors soon discovered ways to make smaller radios. They

ALIEN INVASION!

In 1938 a radio show broadcast a program called *War of the Worlds*. It was a science fiction tale about Martians invading the earth. "Something's wriggling out of the shadow like a gray snake," said an actor playing a newscaster reporting on the Martian invasion. "Now it's another one, and another. They look like tentacles to me. There, I can see the thing's body. It's large as a bear and it glistens like wet leather."

Many listeners thought the show was a real news broadcast. People around the United States panicked. They hid under beds and in basements and crowded the roads, trying to escape the Martian invasion. The broadcast made its director, Orson Welles, very famous.

Special radio broadcast *War of the Worlds* creates a sensation across the United States.

1938

Before cars had CD players and cassette players, they had eight-track players *(right)* in addition to AM/FM radios.

made radios that fit into car dashboards. Then radios got even smaller. People could carry them in one hand or wear them like headphones.

One invention gave radios a better sound. It was a new method of sending radio waves called FM, or frequency modulation. Many FM radio stations began broadcasting in the early 1960s. FM made a big difference to music lovers. It brings a richer, clearer sound to radio. The other kind of radio, AM, or amplitude modulation, doesn't sound as clear.

Radio Calling the Internet, Come In!

Radio is not a new communications technology. But inventors are finding new uses for radio. Wireless computers, for instance, are

Radio signals allow people on earth to hear astronauts speaking on the moon.

1969

equipped with tiny radios that send out and receive radio signals. These signals allow users to connect to the Internet without telephone lines. Wireless connections cut people loose, so they can go online wherever wireless Internet service is available.

RADIO FROM THE STARS

The invention of radio did more than give people an exciting new way of communicating. It also gave astronomers a new tool for studying the universe. In 1931 scientists at the Bell Telephone Laboratories in New Jersey were trying to get rid of static in telephone calls. A scientist named Karl Jansky discovered the cause. It was radio waves from outer space.

No, not from aliens. Stars like our sun send out natural radio signals. Astronomers can capture these signals with big dish-shaped antennae called radio telescopes. These radio signals carry important new information about stars, including how they are born and how they die. The world's largest radio telescope is in Arecibo, Puerto Rico.

CHAPTER 4

Television

A fourteen-year-old high school boy in Idaho had an idea for a great invention. One day he told his science teacher about the idea. The teacher called the boy up to the blackboard and had him sketch out his invention. The teacher smiled. It sounded like science fiction.

That was 1922. People already had the tele*graph*. It sent coded words over wires. They had tele*phones*, which sent voices over wires. They also had radio, which sent voices and music through the air. But this invention was tele*vision*. It would send voices, music, and pictures through the air all at the same time. It would bring lifelike images into boxes in people's living rooms.

The teacher and the boy talked about the idea for weeks. Finally, the teacher decided that it just might work. The boy was Philo T. Farnsworth. And the invention did work. Philo Taylor Farnsworth invented television.

Images through the Air

In the 1920s, many inventors besides Philo Farnsworth were working on developing television. They all had slightly different ideas. However, they all knew that television starts with a camera. The camera scans images, breaking them up into tiny points of light. The light is then changed into electronic signals that travel through the air on radio waves. Then a receiver—a TV set—changes the signals to pictures.

Philo T. Farnsworth

Philo T. Farnsworth sends
the first television image.

1927

The first image that Farnsworth transmitted was a single black line painted on a piece of glass. Workers in his laboratory cheered. That thin line proved that TV would work! It took years to make a television that worked well enough to sell. It also took millions

Two women watch television in 1939. The National Broadcasting Company (owned by RCA) began airing the first regular broadcasts that year. When the United States entered World War II in 1941, however, all television broadcasts were suspended until after the war.

of dollars to pay for the research. The Radio Corporation of America (RCA) spent about fifty million dollars to make television work. Finally, in 1939, RCA started the first regular television broadcasts.

The First TV Sets

The first TV sets were almost the size of refrigerators. They had tiny screens—smaller than a sheet of printer paper. The pictures were unclear. Specks of light drifted across the screen like snow. Screens sometimes showed "ghosts"—double images of people and other objects. All the pictures were black and white.

An early TV set was expensive too. The cheapest one cost about one thousand dollars—as much as a brand-new car cost then. No wonder that by 1950, only nine out of every one hundred homes in the United States had a TV set.

As TVs improved, pictures got clearer, and TV sets got smaller and less expensive. Color television was a big advance. The first color TV sets went on sale in 1954. Americans quickly fell in love with TV. By 1955, 50 percent of all U.S. homes had a television set.

TUNING IN . . . OR OUT?

In the average U.S. home, the TV is turned on more than seven hours a day. In the United States, we spend more time watching TV than doing anything else, except for working, going to school, and sleeping.

Regular television broadcasts begin in the United States.
1939

Color TV becomes available to consumers.
1954

WHAT, NO RERUNS?

The first TV broadcasts were all "live." TV stations broadcast events as they occurred and scenes as the TV stars acted them out. There was no way to record shows. If you missed a TV show, you could never see it again. You could not wait for the reruns because there were none.

In the 1950s, the invention of magnetic videotape changed that. With magnetic tape, TV stations could record news events and entertainment programs. Then the programs could be broadcast at convenient times, when people were home from school or work. The programs could be shown again and again. In modern times, people use DVD and videocassette recorders and TiVo boxes to record their favorite shows and watch them later.

Love That TV

Families that used to gather around the radio for their favorite programs instead began to sit in front of TV sets. Broadcasters turned some of the most popular radio programs into TV shows. One was a comedy and variety show starring actor Milton Berle. The TV version of his show was so popular in the late 1940s and 1950s that some restaurants closed the night it was on—so no one would miss it. Serials, soap operas, comedy shows, sports events, and news broadcasts also made the switch from radio to TV. New kinds of programs appeared. They included game shows and made-for-TV movies.

Making TV More Modern

Scientists continued to improve on television. Cable TV brought

Videotape recording
is invented.
1951

the signal to homes through a cable and gave people more channels to choose from. It caught on in the 1970s. Videocassette recorders allowed people to videotape their favorite programs. Movies on videotape helped turn television sets into home movie screens. The digital video disc (DVD) did even more. It brought sharper pictures and better sounds to TV.

The first VCR models were much larger than the sleek models popular today. Videotapes store images and sound as magnetic impulses that can be played back immediately after recording.

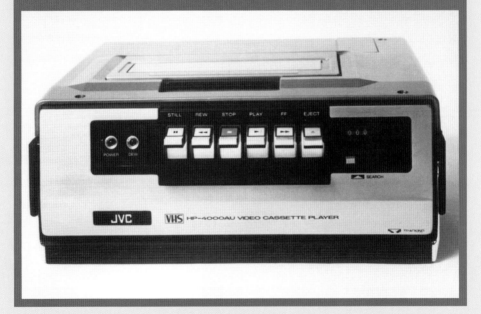

Closed-captioning (text displays on the TV screen) begins in the United States.

1980

Plasma televisions can be mounted on the wall to save space. Plasma displays have a layer of gas between two glass panels. Electricity changes the gas into a special form called a plasma, producing light and color.

By the early 2000s, people were watching better TV pictures. People could watch wide-screen TVs that showed bigger pictures and flat-panel displays that took up less room in the house. TV stations also began broadcasting digital TV, which gives clearer and sharper pictures than regular TV.

TV Changed Life

The invention of TV did much more than just entertain people.

TV became the main way many people learned about the rest of the world. TV puts us at the scene of disasters, wars, and other important events. TV has allowed millions of people to witness great achievements, such as the first humans landing on the moon in 1969. TV has also showed us tragic events, such as the September 11, 2001, terrorist attacks in New York City and near Washington, D.C. TV advertising shows us a dizzying array of products and services. Political ads on television help politicians spread their messages.

Google launches Google Video, which will allow users to search indexed TV show transcripts for key words.

2005

CHAPTER 5

The Internet

The invention of the printing press helped people build huge libraries of books, magazines, and newspapers. The telephone allowed people to talk over long distances. Radio and television brought a whole new world of news and entertainment right into our homes.

The Internet does it all and much more! *Internet* means the *inter*connected *net*work. A network is a series of computers linked together to exchange information. The Internet is the world's biggest computer network. It connects millions of computers using cables, telephone lines, radio signals, and satellite systems. People can connect to the Internet at schools, businesses, government offices, research centers, and homes. Some people can even connect to the Internet using cell phones.

The Internet gives us information on news, weather, and sports. You can read magazine articles and even entire books on the Internet. You can use the Net to watch live TV broadcasts, listen to radio programs, play games, and make telephone calls. Most people who use the Internet send e-mail, or electronic mail. E-mail is a message system that lets people communicate almost instantly with other people anywhere in the world.

FYI: INTERNET SLANG

People using the Internet have invented a new language. It consists of acronyms, or abbreviations, such as FYI, which stands for "for your information." Acronyms are handy for e-mail, chat rooms, and instant messaging. It's easier to keyboard an acronym than to peck out whole words. Here are a few common Internet acronyms:

BTW: by the way
FWIW: for what it's worth
FYI: for your information
HH: holding hands
IAE: in any event
IMHO: in my humble opinion
IOW: in other words
JOOTT: just one of those things
LOL: laughing out loud
NRN: no reply necessary
OTOH: on the other hand
ROF: rolling on the floor (laughing)
TIA: thanks in advance

E-mail is fast becoming one of the most common forms of communication. It is used in schools, businesses, and the home. The Internet handles hundreds of millions of e-mails per day.

Nuke-Proof Communications

The idea for an Internet was invented in 1969 at the U.S. Department of Defense (DOD)—the nation's chief military agency. The military wanted a special communications system that would keep working even if a nuclear attack or another disaster destroyed some of its computers.

The DOD designed a computer network in which every computer could communicate with every other computer. If a few

The U.S. Department of Defense devises an early version of the Internet.

1969

computers were knocked out, the rest could take over. They could route messages around the "dead" computers and keep working. Inventors called this system the ARPAnet, named for DOD's Advanced Research Projects Agency. It was the grandfather of the modern Internet.

In the 1980s, universities and businesses started their own computer networks. People used these networks to exchange

The team that developed the ARPAnet. Many of the men who worked on the project were former Massachusetts Institute of Technology engineers.

information and e-mails with people at the same company or school. In the late 1980s, local computer networks began to connect with one another. They formed the Internet. It began to grow and grow.

Spinning the Web

The Internet really took off in 1989, when British scientist Tim Berners-Lee invented hypertext transfer protocol (http). With this system, Internet users see highlighted words called hypertext on their computer screens. Each highlighted word is linked to more information, often stored in another computer far away. For instance, a

Tim Berners-Lee, inventor of hypertext, outside his Massachusetts Institute of Technology office in 2000

news article about a sporting event might have a hypertext link on a team name. When you click your mouse on that name, the computer jumps to the team's Web page. The new display also has hyperlinks, perhaps to local sports radio shows. By clicking on links, people can navigate a huge amount of information. It's all linked, like the strands on a spider's web. That's where we get the name World Wide Web.

The Internet Revolution

The Internet is having a big effect on everyday life. Students use the Internet to get information for homework assignments. Many people buy products, such as books and CDs, on the Internet. People also use the Internet to make airline and train reservations, book hotel rooms, pay bills, and much more. They use e-mail to ask one another questions, tell stories, and make business deals. And they can do it all without leaving home.

FIGHTING NET NUISANCES

The Internet ran into problems in the late 1990s. Some people created computer "viruses," harmful programs sent over the Internet and e-mail. Viruses can "infect" and damage computers. So inventors had to make new programs to protect computers from viruses. Inventors also created programs that made computers more secure and private—so that outsiders couldn't use the Internet to gain access to personal information stored on computers, such as secret passwords and credit card numbers.

E-commerce, or the buying and selling of goods and services online, is becoming an ever-expanding market. You can do almost anything online, from grocery and clothes shopping to booking vacations to research.

Because of the Internet, some workers no longer need to commute, or travel, to offices every day. Instead, they telecommute. They work from home at a computer and send in their work, such as business plans and reports, by e-mail. Many college professors put their assignments, lectures, and reading lists on the Internet. In this way, students can do their work from home. "Virtual colleges" offer college-level lessons over the Internet.

Blaster, So Big, and other viruses damage millions of computers around the world.

2003

By 2002 approximately 58 percent of the U.S. population had access to the Internet, either at home, school, or work. By 2004 almost 75 percent of U.S. homes had Internet service. The numbers are growing every year. Soon the Internet will be as common in U.S. homes as telephones and televisions.

BAD WEB?

Some scientists worry that the Internet is isolating people from one another. Before the Internet, people had more direct contact with other human beings. They frequently talked to each other, laughed, hugged, and smiled. In the twenty-first century, people punch keyboards and click mouses to communicate. Some experts think that e-mail, chat rooms, instant messaging, and information at your fingertips create a world of lonely people, glued to computer monitors. What do you think?

Epilogue

Years ago, people could only dream of our modern communication technology. E-mail, Internet chat, and cell phones, for instance, once sounded like science fiction. Some upcoming communication technology also sounds fantastic and futuristic—but it's real. Scientists are developing some amazing new devices.

For instance, in the future, your TV might be as big as a shower curtain and made of flexible plastic. You'll be able to hang it on the living room wall, plug it in to watch movies and TV shows, then roll it up when you're not using it. People might use roll-up computer monitors too. A modern flat-screen computer monitor weighs about 15 pounds (6.8 kg). A roll-up monitor may weigh only a few ounces. It would be much easier to carry from one place to another.

Scientists are also developing electronic ink, or e-ink. This new technology uses millions of microscopic, electrically charged particles to create clear, readable text on a surface such as plastic, metal, or paper. The technology allows for the continuous changing of printed information. For example, you wouldn't have to buy a new newspaper each day to read the daily news. Instead, your newspaper would

update itself automatically. Books would never go out of date either. A student might get one electronic book, written with e-ink on flexible pages, at the start of first grade. The student would download new material into the book each year—and use the same book all the way through high school! With only one schoolbook, kids would no longer have to carry heavy backpacks. Fewer trees would have to be cut down to make paper.

Telephones, computers, and other communications devices are already much smaller than they were just ten years ago. And they will continue to get smaller. That's because scientists are finding ways to make electronic chips—the "brains" of computers and other electronic devices—smaller and more powerful. Imagine a cell phone that fits into a ring on your finger. You dial with your voice, by speaking the numbers. It's not science fiction—engineers are already working on the technology.

Scientists are even making computers that you can wear like clothing. The monitors are pairs of special eyeglasses. Imagine using a wearable computer to stay online all day!

A.D. 1045   In China, Bi Sheng invents movable type made of clay.

1440s Johannes Gutenberg develops a printing press with movable type.

1600s The first newspapers are printed in Germany, France, and Belgium.

1791 The First Amendment to the U.S. Constitution provides for freedom of the press.

1831 Michael Faraday discovers that sounds can make wire vibrate.

1837 American inventor Samuel F. B. Morse makes the first usable telegraph.

1850 Samuel Morse invents a code language, Morse code, for use with the telegraph.

1851 The United States has more than fifty telegraph companies.

1860s James Clerk Maxwell predicts the existence of radio waves.

1873 A gun manufacturer called E. Remington and Sons produces the first widely sold typewriter.

1876 Alexander Graham Bell patents the first telephone.

1884 Ottmar Mergenthaler invents the Linotype machine.

1888 Heinrich Hertz discovers that an electric spark sends radio waves into space.

1895 Nikola Tesla invents a coil that can transmit radio waves for 50 miles (80 km).

1901 Guglielmo Marconi sends the first transatlantic radio message between Great Britain and Canada.

1904 Inventors create offset printing.

1912 *Carpathia* receives a radio message from the sinking *Titanic* and speeds to the scene to rescue survivors.

1920 Station KDKA in Pittsburgh, Pennsylvania, makes the first commercial radio broadcast.

1927 Philo T. Farnsworth develops the first all-electric television image.

1931 Karl Jansky at Bell Telephone Laboratories discovers that stars emit radio waves.

1938 Special radio broadcast *War of the Worlds* creates a sensation across the United States.

1939 RCA starts regular television broadcasts.

1950 About 75 percent of all phone lines in the United States are party lines, with many customers sharing one line.

1951 The first long-distance calls using area codes are placed. Videotape recording is invented.

1954 The first color television sets go on sale in the United States.

1955 Approximately 50 percent of homes in the United States have a television set.

1969 The U.S. Department of Defense (DOD) develops the ARPAnet computer network.

1976 Queen Elizabeth of Great Britain is the first world leader to use e-mail.

1980s The Internet replaces ARPAnet.

1989 Tim Berners-Lee develops hypertext links.

1995 Caller ID becomes available in the United States.

1996 About 45 million people are using the Internet for information and communication.

2002 About 58 percent of the U.S. population has Internet access.

2005 More than 170 million cell phones are in use in the United States. Google launches Google Video, which will allow users to search indexed TV show transcripts for key words.

GLOSSARY

broadcast: to transmit information by radio or television

cell phone: a portable, cordless telephone that allows people to talk and send messages using radio waves

chip: a tiny piece of material containing a complex electronic circuit

e-mail: a system for sending written messages through a computer network; short for "electronic mail"

hypertext transfer protocol (http): a system that allows users to navigate the Internet via a series of linked words, or hypertext

Internet: an electronic network that links computers around the world

letterpress printing: a printing method that involves creating images by pressing paper against an inked surface

media: the communications industry, including television, radio, and newspapers, designed to reach a large audience

movable type: metal blocks bearing numbers, letters, or other characters that can be arranged and rearranged for printing words and sentences

offset printing: a printing process in which an inked image is transferred onto a rubber-coated cylinder and then onto paper

optical fibers: thin, transparent glass or plastic threads used to transmit telephone calls

patent: a government document that gives someone the right to make and sell a new invention

radio telescopes: powerful antennae that can receive natural radio signals from outer space

radio waves: invisible, naturally occurring waves that can carry electrical current through the air

satellite: a space vehicle that receives radio, television, and other signals in space and relays them back to earth

telegraph: a system for sending coded electrical signals over wires

viruses: computer programs that reproduce themselves and "infect" other programs, often causing damage to computer systems

World Wide Web: the worldwide network of websites and Web pages connected by hyperlink text

Source Notes

17 "American Treasures of the Library of Congress: Reason," *Library of Congress*, 2003, http://www.loc.gov/exhibits/treasures/trr002.html (April 15, 2005).

27 "Spielberg and Cruise Plan New War of Worlds," *Guardian Unlimited*, March 18, 2004, http://www.guardian.co.uk/international/story/0,,1171888,00.html (June 13, 2005).

Bibliography

Berners-Lee, Tim. *Weaving the Web: The Original Design and Ultimate Destiny of the World Wide Web by Its Inventor.* New York: Harper Collins, 2000.

Brockman, John. *The Greatest Inventions of the Past 2,000 Years.* New York: Simon and Schuster, 2000.

Dyson, James. *A History of Great Inventions.* New York: Carroll and Graf Publishers, 2001.

Harrison, Peter. *All about Inventions: Amazing Breakthroughs That Shaped Our World.* London: Anness Publishing, Ltd., 2000.

Schwartz, Evan I. *The Last Lone Inventor: Tale of Genius, Deceit, and the Birth of Television.* New York: Harper Collins, 2002.

Weightman, Gavin. *Signor Marconi's Magic Box.* Cambridge, MA: Da Capo Press, 2003.

FURTHER READING AND WEBSITES

Barasch, Lynne. *Radio Rescue*. New York: Farrar, Straus and Giroux, 2000.
This story takes place in 1923, when a ten-year-old boy uses his wireless
radio receiver to answer a call for help and rescues a family from a hurricane.

Burch, Joann Johansen. *Fine Print: A Story about Johannes Gutenberg*.
Minneapolis: Lerner Publications Company, 1991.
Burch uses a story format to introduce Gutenberg, the inventor of the
printing press.

Communication-Related Inventors and Inventions
http://www.enchantedlearning.com/inventors/communication.shtml
This wonderful site has information about every inventor who had
anything to do with communication.

Computers and the Internet
http://www.factmonster.com/ipka/A0772279.html
Information Please developed this site, and it is filled with amazing facts
about computers and the World Wide Web.

Graham, Ian. *Techworld: Computers*. New York: Raintree Steck-Vaughn, 2001.
Techworld explains the workings of computers, their original uses, and their
many modern applications.

Information Age: People, Information, and Technology
http://photo2.si.edu/infoage/infoage.html
The National Museum of American History at the Smithsonian Institution
provides photos from its Information Age exhibit.

Internet Glossary
http://www.education-world.com/help/glossary.shtml
Visitors can find a glossary of commonly used Internet terms on this site.

Johannes Gutenberg
http://www.ideafinder.com/history/inventors/gutenberg.htm
This website provides information about Johannes Gutenberg, who developed the technique of using movable type to print multiple copies of text.

Krensky, Stephen. *Breaking into Print: Before and after the Invention of the Printing Press*. Boston: Little, Brown and Co., 1996.
This book gives a historical account of the world before the invention of the printing press.

Mattern, Joanne. *The Printing Press: An Information Revolution*. New York: Power Kids Press, 2003.
In this book, you can learn about the development of the printing press.

———. *Television: Window to the World*. New York: Power Kids Press, 2003.
This book explains the history and influence of television on modern society.

McPherson, Stephanie Sammartino. *TV's Forgotten Hero: The Story of Philo. T. Farnsworth*. Minneapolis, Carolrhoda Books, Inc., 1996.
Learn all about the man who worked so hard to make his idea of television a reality.

Sherman, Josepha. *The History of the Internet*. New York: Franklin Watts, 2003.
This book provides an easy introduction to and explanation of the Internet.

Tagliaferro, Linda. *Thomas Edison: Inventor of the Age of Electricity*. Minneapolis: Lerner Publications Company, 2003.
This biography details the life of one of the world's greatest inventors.

Ten Commandments for Computer Ethics
http://www.tekmom.com/tencommand/index.html
You can learn your Internet manners here.

Time-Life Books. *Inventive Genius*. Alexandria, VA: Time-Life Books, 1991.
Inventive Genius describes the invention of Velcro, the leotard, telephones, radios, video games, and correction fluid.

Woods, Michael, and Mary B. Woods. *Ancient Communication: From Grunts to Graffiti*. Minneapolis: Runestone Press, 2000.
This book provides an overview of communication in the ancient world.

Cover and Chapter Opener Photo Captions

Cover Top: Alexander Graham Bell *(left)* and Thomas Watson *(right)* examine Bell's first telephone. Bottom: People use cell phones to communicate in many different ways.

pp. 4–5 Newspapers roll off a printing press in the 1930s.

p. 6 A scribe writes out Hebrew script. Before printing presses, books had to be written by hand with quill and ink.

p. 14 A switchboard operator in the early twentieth century conects calls.

p. 22 Actors rehearse for a radio drama in the 1920s.

p. 30 A family watches a favorite television program in the 1950s.

p. 38 A group of schoolchildren learn about Australia on the Internet.

pp. 46–47 A South Korean man shows off a small wearable computer.

About the Authors

Michael Woods is a science and medical journalist who has won many national writing awards. Mary B. Woods has worked as a librarian in the Fairfax County Public School System in Virginia and at the Benjamin Franklin International School in Barcelona, Spain. The Woodses' previous books include an eight-volume Ancient Technology series.

Photo Acknowledgments

The images in this book are used with the permission of: © BBC/CORBIS, pp. 4–5; Courtesy Museum of the Alphabet, p. 6; © Bettmann/CORBIS, pp. 9, 25, 28, 35; Mergenthaler Linotype Co., p. 11; Minnesota Historical Society, p. 14; © CORBIS, p. 15; © Jose Luis Pelaez, Inc./CORBIS, pp. 19, 36; © age fotostock/SuperStock, p. 21; © Schenectady Museum; Hall of Electrical History Foundation/CORBIS, pp. 22, 32; Library of Congress, pp. 23 (LC-DIG-ggbain-04851), 24 (LC-USZ62-107409); © SuperStock, Inc./SuperStock, pp. 26, 30; Special Collections Dept., J. Willard Marriott Library, University of Utah, p. 31; © Michael L. Abramson/Time Life Pictures/Getty Images, p. 38; © Raymond Forbes/SuperStock, p. 40; Courtesy Bolt, Beranek & Newman, p. 41; © Ed Quinn/CORBIS, p. 42; © Ed Bock/CORBIS, p. 44; © Chung Sung-Jun/Getty Images, pp. 46–47.

Front cover: top, © CORBIS; bottom, © Val Huselid/Independent Picture Service. Montgomery Ward & Co., back cover, p. 1, all borders.